CAMOUFLAGE & MARKINGS
Luftwaffe 1939~1945

Compiled by

Mike Reynolds

Assisted by
Bernie McCartney
Guy Reynolds

Argus Books

ARGUS BOOKS
Argus House
Boundary Way
Hemel Hempstead
Herts HP2 7ST
England

First published by Argus Books 1992
© Argus Books 1992

ISBN 1 85486 066 6

Phototypesetting by
Island Graphics, Chesham.
Printed and bound in Great Britain by William
Clowes Ltd., Beccles.

Introduction

IT IS not the intention of this book to give an in-depth appraisal of the technical details, nor a concise history or performance analysis of the various aircraft illustrated. There are far more qualified people who have already covered this area of research in many other volumes, some in great detail.

My purpose is to draw and describe for the modeller some of the most modelled aircraft of World War Two, giving a good basic set of information on the so-called standard colours and markings set out by the various Government departments controlling aircraft production. There were, of course, thousands of variations, deviations and other oddities brought about by the vagaries of wear and tear in the front line and even training units, the difficulties of war-time production, repair and supply, or in some instances simple variations brought about by the personal preferences of individuals or units.

In many cases, aircraft units and sometimes pilots can be identified by such markings and badges whilst, in some notable cases, individual units are identifiable by their own modifications to the issued camouflaged machines.

You can see, therefore, that this small volume can only provide a base of limited data for a selected few aircraft, although I hope that the modeller, whether working on static solid scale and plastic or flying scale models, will be able to produce a presentable representative miniature from the information found here. However, for specific subjects there can be no substitution for in-depth, detailed and cross-referenced research, especially in reference to good quality photographs which are to be found in many magazines and books specialising on specific periods, air forces, campaigns, and aircraft. These can often be quite costly, so a visit to your local library is recommended.

I often find cheap books on aircraft on stalls at airshows, whilst a visit to your local model shop could prove fruitful, and friends are often a good source. However, beware of relying too much on line drawing and artwork, some of which is highly dubious, especially that which was produced some years ago, whilst many scale drawings, even recent productions, have inaccuracies. In fact, accurate drawings are quite rare.

When consulting your colour photographs, it must be kept in mind that the accurate reproduction from some film emulsions of the period is not as good as that produced by modern technology, whilst others have deteriorated with age. Varying light conditions also have dramatic results on the published product, as can frequently be seen in currently published periodicals. There is the renowned example of a squadron of Mustangs, long thought of as painted blue on their upper surfaces, which actually turned out to be standard olive green on research and correction in the reproduction. Memory can be just as fallible. For instance, the example of the P51 Mustang 'Milli G', which the pilot recalled painted scarlet and which was produced in kit form to reflect this was later found to have been finished in the standard olive drab finish. However, modern technology and research have made great improvements in elimination of these errors and I hope the colour chips and drawings will help you in producing a more accurate finish.

One last consideration in this modelling minefield is that of scale colour. With the distance between the viewer and the subject increasing, the actual intensity of colour pales. This phenomenon has long been exploited by the artist, especially in landscape painting, to give a sense of depth to the work. A school of thought in modelling circles believes that the discipline in art should be applied to modelling work. A 1/72nd scale model viewed at the optimum distance of 12" represents looking at a full-size object at a distance of about 100ft. It should, according to this school of thought, be paler in colour than if the object is viewed at a close distance. The recommended colour mix is quoted as 40% white to 60% basic colour to give a representative toned down hue, whilst for other scales the proportions of white to colour must be adjusted accordingly, but the results are entirely to the liking of the builder. Experiment a little until you find a finish that is pleasing to you, and balance this with a little wear and tear weathering for the final acceptable result.

The Junkers Ju87 'Stuka'

The Ju87 Stuka was literally a piece of precision flying artillery, and it epitomises the flawed thinking that dominated Luftwaffe strategy in the early War years and which ultimately contributed to Germany's defeat.

The German High Command saw no requirement for a strategic offensive capability, regarding their air force merely as a supportive tactical force for the army and the Blitzkrieg tactics. In this role, throughout its career, over the Low Countries and Poland in 1940, in the North African deserts, and over the vast Russian steppes, the aircraft was superlative. It was, however, very vulnerable to air interception, especially at the beginning or when pulling out of a dive, and the type suffered badly at the hands of the RAF during the Luftwaffe's air offensive over the UK in 1940.

The Stuka was to enjoy further success when deployed in North Africa, in the Balkans Campaign, where it was also used by the Italians, and against the convoys supplying the island of Malta.

It was on the Eastern Front, however, that the aircraft was to enjoy its greatest successes. The B type was joined by the radically-improved D variant. It added to its pinpoint bombing attributes by becoming an outstanding tank destroyer, but the fortunes of the type were in decline, for the Luftwaffe was losing control of the air on all fronts and the Stuka found it increasingly difficult to operate under such conditions. It was finally withdrawn completely at the end of 1944.

Many illustrations depict the Ju87 with a single green top colour. This is incorrect, and is probably caused by reference to photographs which do not show up the low contrast between Grün 71 and Schwarz Grün 70.

The first side view shows a Ju87B aircraft from Gruppe Stab of 1/stg1. The individual letter A is in white, but it would normally have been in blue or green for a Stab Flight machine. Illustration two shows the Russian Front. The aircraft is still in two greens but the yellow theatre markings dominate the finish. We now turn to North Africa where white replaces yellow as the theatre marking and a Sandgelb 69, blotched with 80 Olivgrün. The final D version serving on the Eastern Front has the standard scheme oversprayed with a 'mirror wave' wavy white line on all top surfaces and spats.

MG 15

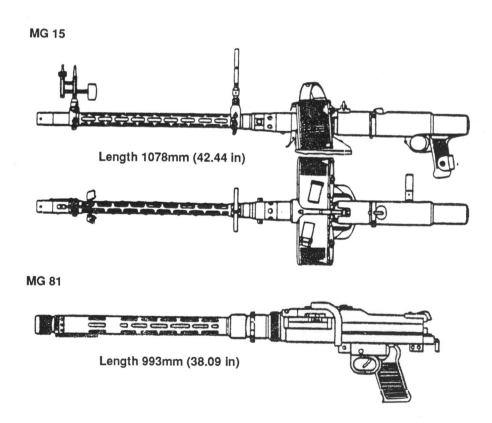

Length 1078mm (42.44 in)

MG 81

Length 993mm (38.09 in)

4

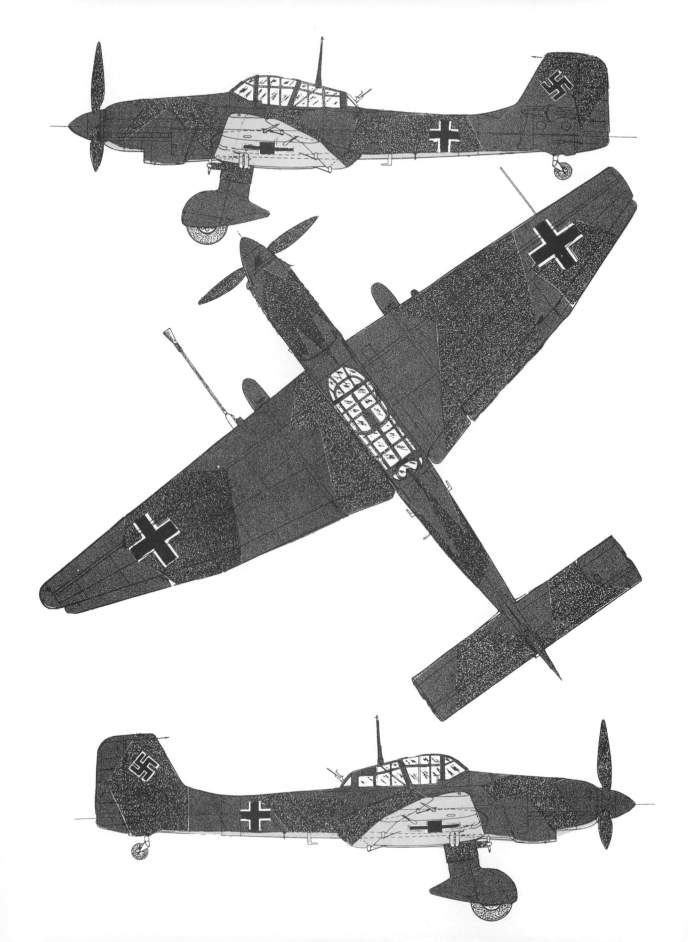

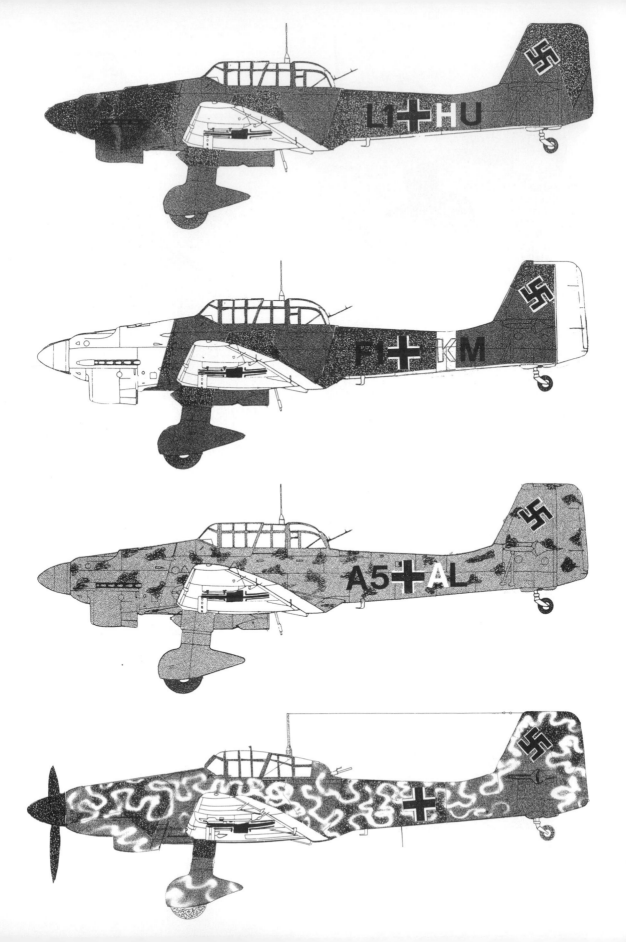

The Messerschmitt bf 109e and f

The ME bf109 was the mainstay of Germany's fighter effort throughout the Second World War, and was produced in greater numbers than any other aircraft of that War. It first flew a little earlier than either of its major opponents – the Spitfire and Hurricane – and entered service before either of them. It was largely evaluated under service conditions when flying with the Condor Legion during the Spanish Civil War.

By the time War broke out, the improved e version was rolling off the production lines and was deployed most successfully in the tactics developed in Spain. Despite the myth and legend surrounding the Battle of Britain, the 109 equipped itself admirably, having a better score to loss ratio than either of its opponents.

Despite this success, shortfalls in the aircraft's performance were recognised by the design team who undertook a major improvement programme. This produced what was probably the definitive version, the f variant, which, with its revised nose contours, rounded wing tips and strengthened tail unit eliminating the e's bracing struts, retained the earlier mark's light handling properties with some of the increase in power, speed, range and firepower of the yet-to-come marks.

The three-view drawing depicts a machine as it should have been finished in 70/71/65 colours in early 1940. By the early summer, instructions had been issued to raise the blue well up the fuselage sides to give the 'classic' Battle of Britain image. However, several aircraft are recorded as having the Grün 70 replaced by Graü 02, or even both greens replaced by Graü 74/75. Many units found the Blau 65 fuselage sides not to their liking, and brought varying styles and colours down over the base colour.

Side view one is of the classic 'e' in Battle of Britain markings, while serving with Stab/JG2 in August 1940. The second drawing is also classic, in that it shows the field modification of sprayed lattice work over the the lower 65 Hellblau, and readily identifies the aircraft as belonging to JG54. Other units had their own variations.

The 109 was widely used on the Russian Front, and the third drawing shows the aircraft with the campaign's yellow wing tip, under nose and tailband. This was an extension to the yellow noses seen over England in 1940, which were not flamboyant squadron colours but applied as recognition aids in anticipation of the proposed invasion.

Our fourth view shows an f serving in the desert in a plain two-colour finish, with white recognition markings. In some cases, yellow was retained for this purpose.

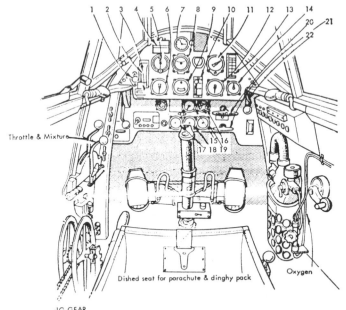

Throttle & Mixture

Dished seat for parachute & dinghy pack

Oxygen

JG GEAR

1	Cut off switch	8	Compass	15	Oil Pressure
2	Gun selector	9	Turn & Bank	16	U/C Indicator
3	Heater control	10	Propeller pitch selector	17	Fuel
4	Data Card	11	Boost guage	18	Oil Temp.
5	Altimeter	12	R.P.M.	19	Rad. Temp.
6	Air speed	13	Deviation table	20 & 21	U/C Selectors
7	Clock	14	Rate of Climb	22	Hand pump

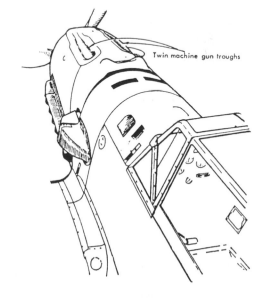

Twin machine gun troughs

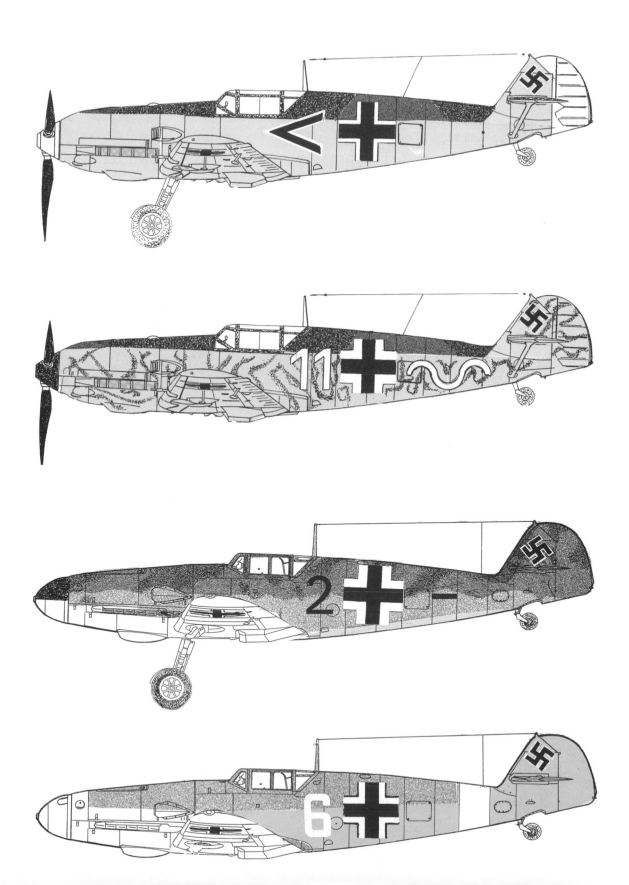

Messerschmitt Me110

At the outbreak of War, the Luftwaffe's Me110 was regarded as the elite of the air arm. It was thought that its heavy firepower and high top speed would either allow it to blast a path for the bomber force through any protective air umbrella, or to outpace any pursuing fighter. This view proved to be flawed in the air battles over England, when the type was shown not to be fast enough to elude the Spitfires and Hurricanes nor aerobatic enough to be able to dogfight with them.

The 'Zerstorer' was to redeem itself later when, with great success, it took on the night fighter defence role in the face of a steadily growing British offensive. For this task, the aircraft was fitted with a succession of steadily improving radar sets. It was also fitted with 'Schrage Musik' upward firing cannon, or machine gun batteries designed to fire upwards at an angle of 65 degrees into the unprotected belly of the enemy bomber, and mounted in the cockpit between the pilot and crewman. This innovation, never fully suspected by the British, proved very effective, if very noisy!

The 110 was still employed in daylight operations over the vast tracts of Russia and the North African desert and, so hard-pressed were the daylight defences of the Reich, it was used occasionally against the massed formations of American bombers. However, such sorties became virtually suicidal and the type was gradually replaced.

Serving throughout the duration of the War in both the day and night fighting roles, the Me 110 initially wore a large range of colour schemes, and, as shown in the three-view drawing, the splinter style in the same colours as the bombers it was intended to escort. However, these colours were rapidly changed as for the 109 with RLM02 often replacing Schwarzgrün RLM70. The top side view shows the initial two green scheme, but with the underside blue extending well up the fuselage sides to end in a soft 'line' when the aircraft served with ZG2, in France 1946. The second side view shows a later style of marking with light grey dappled over with the darker RLM 74.

The third view shows an E-1 serving in North Africa with a mirror wave in Olivgrün over Sandgelb. Our final side view shows a G-4 night fighter in late War soft edge splinter style camouflage and late greens 80/81.

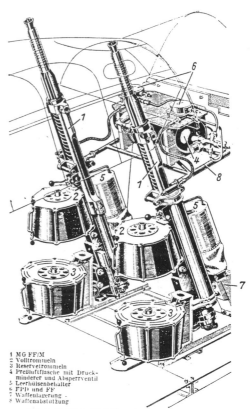

Detail from Official handbook shows Messerschmitt Bf 110 G-4/R fitted with two 20 mm MG FF/M cannon in the co-called Schrage Musik (Jazz Music) installation. Mounting is in the rear cockpit, facing forward.

1 MG FF/M
2 Volltrommeln
3 Reservetrommeln
4 Preßluftflasche mit Druck-
  minderer und Absperrventil
5 Leerhülsenbehälter
6 FPD und FF
7 Waffenlagerung .
8 Waffenabstützung

Abb. 6: Bf 110 G-4/R 8 Übersicht MG-FF/M Schrägeinbau

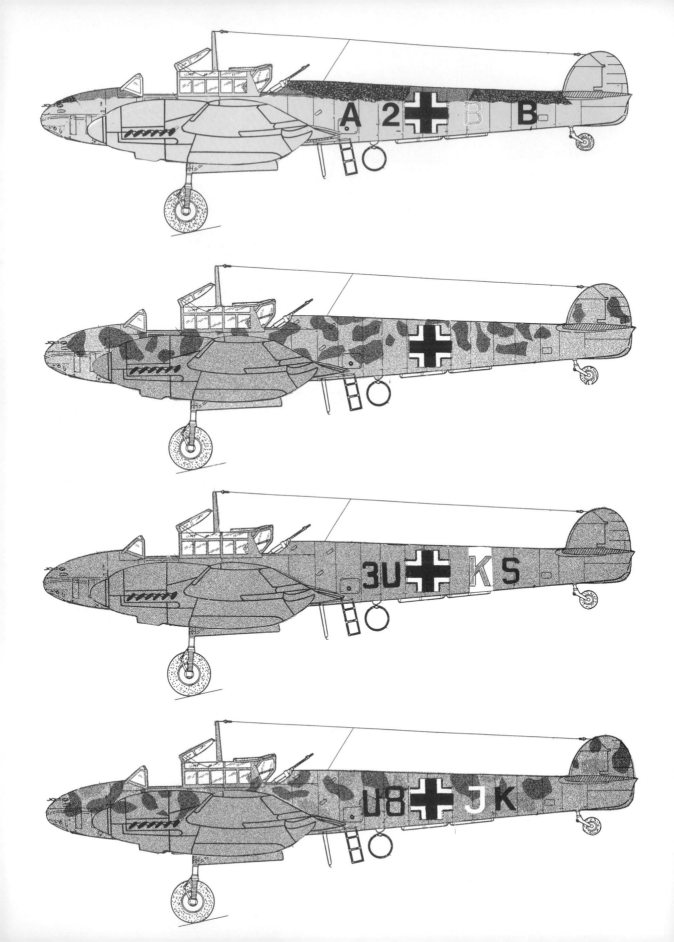

Dornier Do17

Nicknamed 'The Flying Pencil' because of its very slim fuselage shape, the Dornier was originally introduced in the guise of a high speed mailplane and executive civilian transport. It was, in fact, offered to Lufthansa as such, but as proposed passengers would need to be contortionists to get into their seats, it was rejected. This disguise disappeared when the aircraft was displayed at Zurich in 1937, when it outpaced all the opposition – even fighters – to everyone's concern.

At the outbreak of War, several variants were in service, both in bomber and reconnaissance roles, including the M version with BMW in-line engines that had been intended to fill the export market.

The type met with limited success, however, and its light armament and light bomb load were beginning to show up as liabilities but, as there were no plans for replacement, the type would have to remain in service for most of the War, not only fulfilling its existing roles but taking on night fighting and anti-shipping operations, which went far beyond realistic consideration if success were to be assured.

To its credit, the Dornier did better than expected and is even recorded as making the first attack with a guided missile against an enemy warship. It must be considered one of the most important types in the Luftwaffe wartime inventory and, despite not having the versatility of the Ju88 or being produced in the same quantity as the He111, it provided a substantial third pillar of strength to the German air offensive.

Once again the three-view drawing depicts the standard bomber scheme. However, some Do17's saw the opening of the German offensive against Poland still wearing the original three colour pre-War camouflage, shown in the first view.

Kg 77 bore the brunt of much of the fighting until late 1941. The aircraft depicted in the second view shows an aircraft lost by this unit near Dover in July 1940.

The third view shows a Do17p photo-reconnaissance variant liberally applied on the underside with black distemper obscuring both unity and national markings. The final side view shows an aircraft operating on the Eastern Front and bearing the yellow Russian front wing tips, rudders and fuselage band.

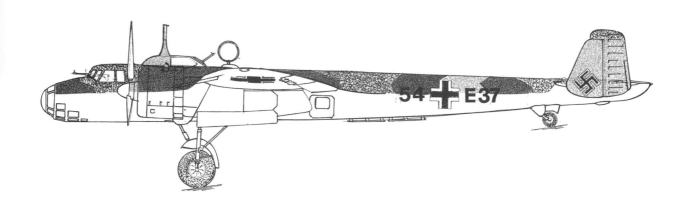

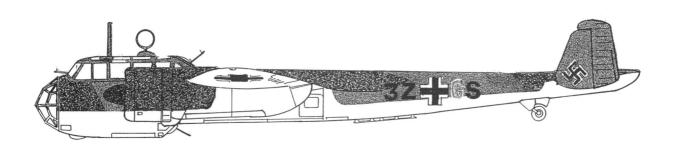

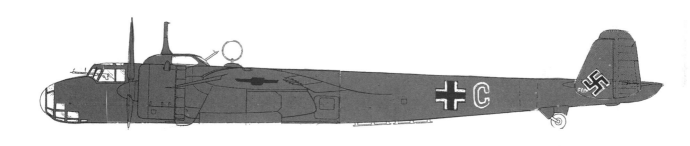

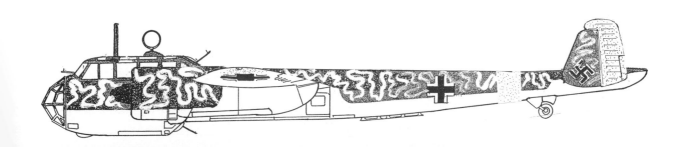

The Heinkel He III

The He III was one of the three major bomber types deployed by the Luftwaffe during World War Two and, despite being due for replacement on at least two occasions, continued in large-scale production for almost the entire conflict.

Like several other German types, the aircraft was baptised into combat during the Spanish Civil War, where several shortcomings in power, etc, came to light and were corrected, changing the more conventional stepped-nose configuration for an entire glazed, shark-like front end.

The aircraft was mass deployed on the invasion of Poland, and again in the assault on the Low Countries, where it gained a good deal of success. It was flown in fairly large formations against targets well behind the somewhat fluid front lines, causing substantial destruction to cities and industrial targets and to civilian morale.

It was during the Battle of Britain that the type was to meet its match, when its cruising speed of just over 200 mph, light armament and standard bomb load of some 5000 lb were all to prove inadequate. Despite being ever more closely escorted by the Me109e and Me110 fighters, the Heinkel suffered considerable losses. The Luftwaffe was forced to operate by night and, while the He111 proved more suitable for this type of mission, its relatively light bomb load would continue to be a drawback that would never be fully overcome.

All bombers were finished in black green/green splinter for at least the first half of the War and, generally speaking, throughout, although some changes did begin to appear late in the conflict. More appropriate colours and schemes were used in North Africa. The three views show the more standard pattern, which is also reflected in side view one of an aircraft during the Battle of Britain from Kg53 'Grifen' Bomb Group, Villacoublay, France.

Lack of success forced the Luftwaffe into night bombing in the autumn of 1940, and the undersides of the majority of participating bombers were painted in a soluble black emulsion, which needed to be cleaned off and replaced every two weeks or so. This aircraft is from Kg55.

The third view is of an aircraft used by the Franco-German Armistice Commission in North Africa, ostensibly as civil transport, hence the civilian codes. But it was still armed! The fourth view is of a very patchy torpedo-carrying aircraft. The top surface shows a heavy mottle in 80 Olivgrün and 81 Braunviolett over 78 Himmelblau.

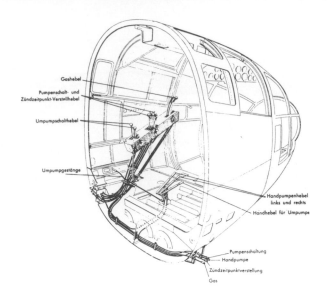

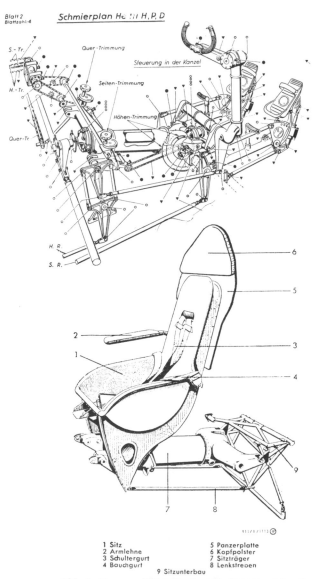

1 Sitz
2 Armlehne
3 Schultergurt
4 Bauchgurt
9 Sitzunterbau
5 Panzerplatte
6 Kopfpolster
7 Sitzträger
8 Lenkstreben

Abb. 8: Flugzeugführersitz (angehoben gezeichnet)

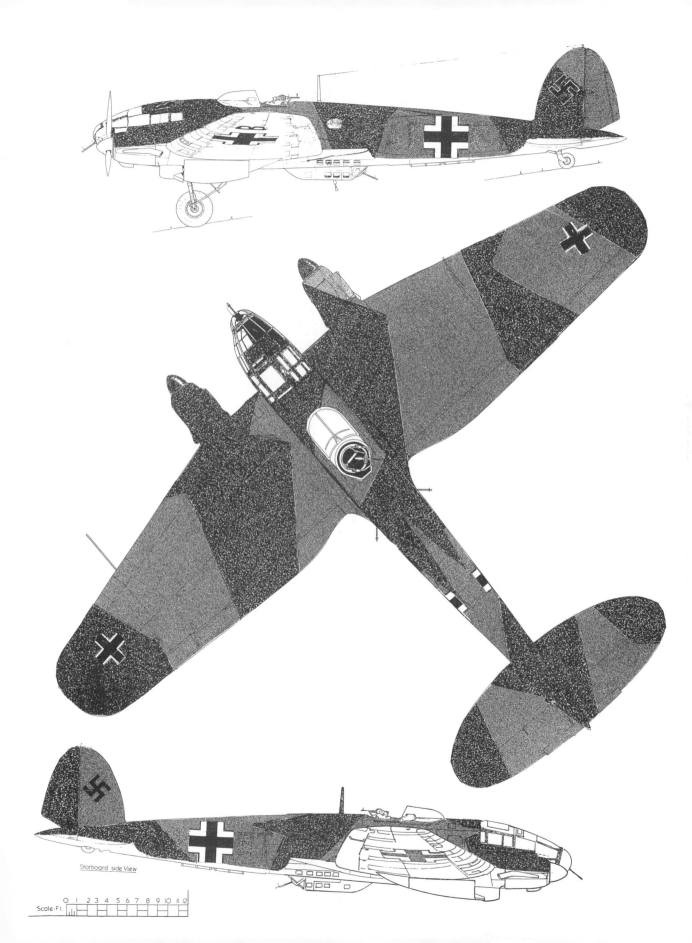

Starboard side View

Scale·Ft 0 1 2 3 4 5 6 7 8 9 10 11 12

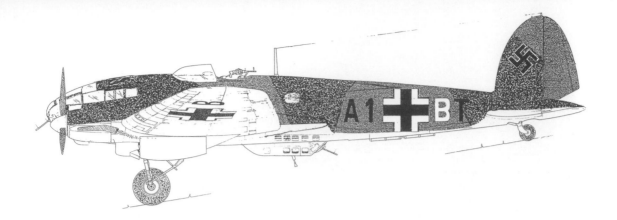

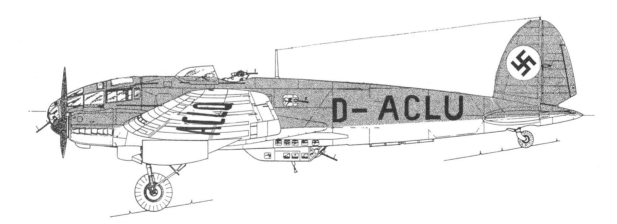

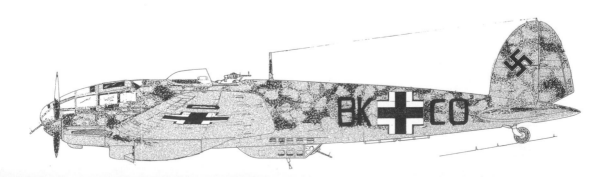

Junkers Ju 88

Of all of the excellent combat aircraft used by the Axis Powers, indeed of any airforce during the Second World War, the Ju 88 must rank amongst the best. It must have been the most modified and developed airframe ever built, for the final derivative – the Ju 488 – bore practically no resemblance to the basic type, having two fins and overall dimensions some 50% larger than the original.

Introduced as a medium/dive bomber during the winter of 1939/40, the Ju 88 was the most successful German type during the early War years and it was rapidly developed for a number of alternative tasks, such as night and intruder fighter, anti-shipping and even anti-tank and ground attack duties, all of which it fulfilled most successfully. So diverse were the roles the aircraft was now asked to take on, that separate design facilities for the development of each type were set up to work in parallel, resulting in the R and S series plus the 188, 288, and 388.

The aircraft was lengthened, strengthened, and fitted with increasingly sophisticated radar and heavier calibre weapons. It was pressurised, given a large internal bomb bay, fitted with an anti-tank cannon and hung with a torpedo. While all of these had a detrimental effect on the basic design, the aircraft was still a firm favourite until the very end. It was fortunate that the original design was so sound, as it provided a successful basis for such diverse major development, which has never really been equalled.

The Ju 88, in its initial bomber version, was delivered in a standard two green splinter bomber pattern, shown in the three views and again in the top side view which shows an A1 sub type serving with II/KG 51 and shot down by Hurricanes on 7th Oct 1940.

Side view two shows this basic scheme adapted for the Mediterranean theatre with the application of white fuselage bands. This would be further modified with an application of a white wavy line for operation over the water, as shown.

The third view shows the light dapple grey finish applied to night fighter variants.

Temporary white paint was not limited to the Eastern Front; this S1 variant was captured by the British in the winter of 1944 and has a liberal application of brushed-on blotches illustrated in the fourth and final side illustration.

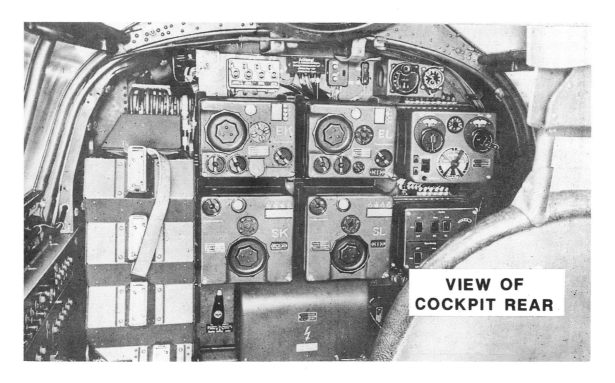

VIEW OF COCKPIT REAR

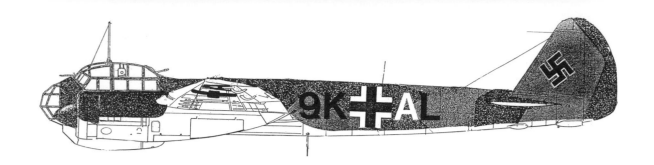

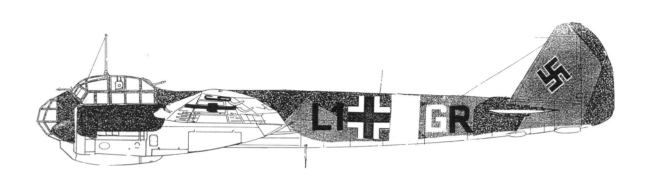

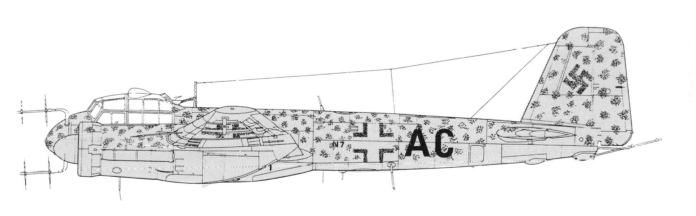

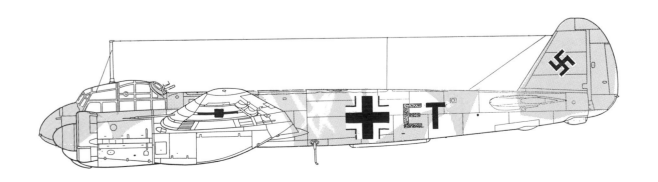

FW 190

The arrival of Focke-Wulf's 'Butcher Bird' in the skies over Northern Europe coincided with the final changes to the initial official fighter colour scheme, and the first operational machines were delivered in RLM02/71 top colours over 65 undersides and applied in a soft-edged splinter style. This contrasted with the sharply defined demarcation normally used up to that time, but which became more prevalent on all types as the conflict progressed.

The top view shows an early aircraft in these colours serving with JG26, the first unit operational on the type.

The second side view shows an aircraft from 111/JG2 in 1942, showing a typical example of unit applied markings which, therefore, were unique to that unit and helped with unit identification - in this case not only because of the unit emblem of a cock's head painted on the engine cowl but through the stylised eagles painted on the fuselage sides to minimise the discolouration caused by exhaust stains.

Another unit readily identified via its individual paint schemes was JG54, who painted their aircraft with large blotches of colour, many of them non-standard and therefore will not be found in the individual RLM colour listing. Such a scheme is shown in side view three.

The fourth view shows the 3-grey scheme RLM 74/75/76 applied later in the War complete with the specified black and white spiral painted on the spinner.

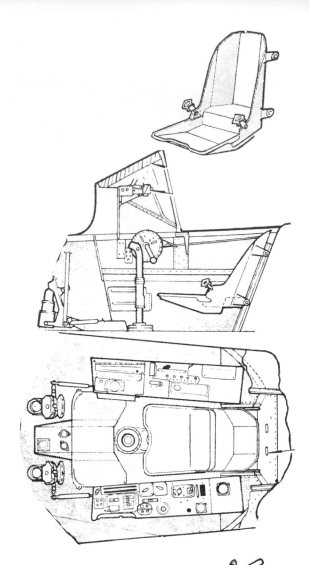

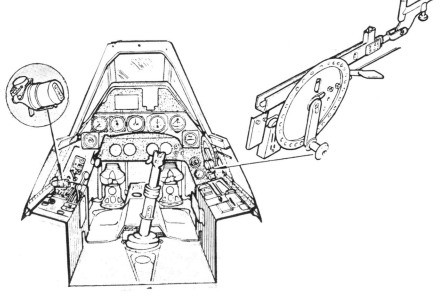

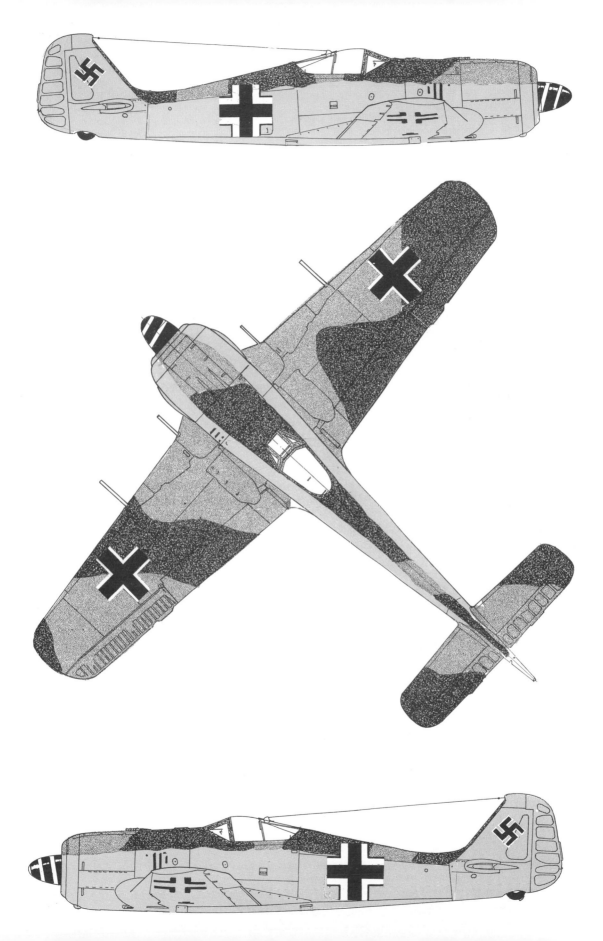

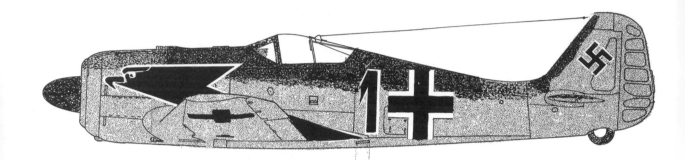

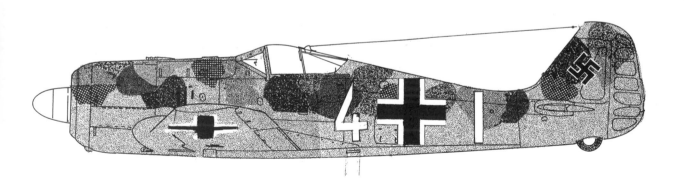

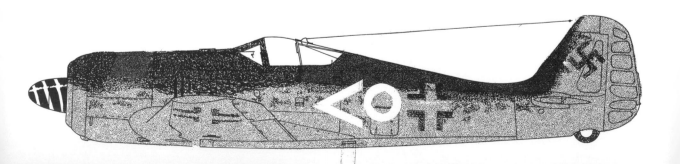

Henschel Hs 129

This heavily armoured and armed twin engine ground attack aircraft had been designed to relieve the Ju 87D 'Stuka' of much of its workload by providing an effective ground attack/anti-armour type and for close support for the ground forces.

Because the aircraft suffered serious deficiencies throughout its career, being underpowered and having poor handling problems compounded by maintenance difficulties which were never fully resolved, it is doubtful that, under less stressful conditions or in any other Air Force, the machine would have been accepted. In fact, it never managed to match or replace the older dive bomber.

The prototype had been fitted with Argus in-line engines of some 450hp, which gave the aircraft a theoretical speed of 225mph, a speed rarely achieved. The French-built Gnome Rhone radial engines were chosen for the production machine but the aircraft was still limited by power levels and the engines had a poor serviceability record. Production was abandoned in early 1944 after 866 machines had been built.

The three-view drawings are of the standard RLM scheme in Grün 70/71 with 65 Blau underside. In the first view, although the aircraft was not a great success some pilots did achieve successes with the type. This aircraft belonged to 8 (Pz) SG1 and was flown by Rudolf-Heinz Ruffer who had more than 70 enemy tanks to his credit. With the onset of the Russian winter, the majority of German aircraft received a coat of white distemper to various degrees. The aircraft depicted in the second view, from 8/SCHG1 in the winter of early 1943, is almost entirely covered, with the exception of squadron and national markings and the yellow theatre of operation areas.

The third view shows the version of the aircraft carrying the giant 75mm anti-tank cannon. This aircraft in the standard scheme served with Gruppe Stab N (Pz) SG9 in late 1944.

The final view is of an unidentified unit operating in Libya. It is finished in the standard Sandgelb 79 over spray on all top surfaces in Olivgrün RLM 80 and undersides in Hellblau RLM Shade 78. Other machines had plain top sides.

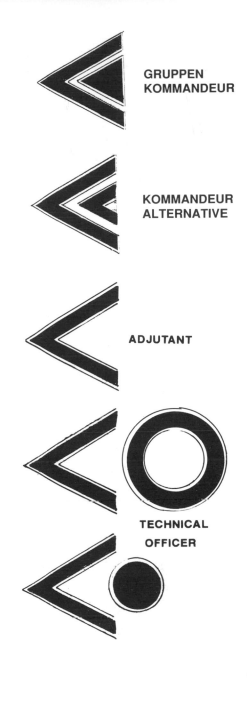

GRUPPEN KOMMANDEUR

KOMMANDEUR ALTERNATIVE

ADJUTANT

TECHNICAL OFFICER

FIGHTER GRUPPEN PILOT RANK MARKINGS CARRIED FORWARD OF NATIONAL MARKINGS

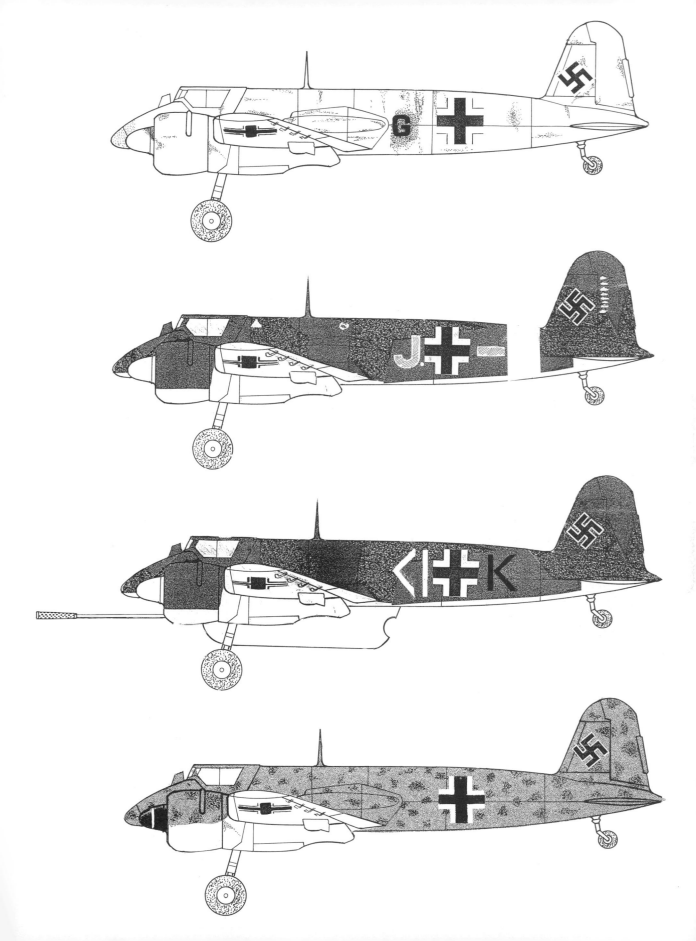

The Messerschmitt Me 109g and k

Following the definitive 'f' variant of the 109, Germany was still in need of large numbers of defensive fighters to meet the growing threat imposed by new and improved fighter opposition. Proposed replacements had proven disappointing, and production of the FW190 could not meet the increasing needs. Therefore, it became necessary to carry on developing the 109, even though it was generally considered that, with the f series, the aircraft had reached its optimum in development.

The most important change in the aircraft, with the introduction of the g series in late 1943, was the incorporation of the DB601 engine and also the incorporation of pressurisation to cope with the increasing altitudes at which combats were now taking place.

The final version, the 'k', was an attempt to put all of the hotchpotch of improvements spread over the main g sub variants into one new fresh development, to assist with production and maintenance and to redress some of the loss in handling qualities. But only a small number reached operational status.

The three-view drawing depicts one of what appear to be four basic camouflage patterns applied to the later marks in RLM 74/75/76 colours and, although distinct in shape, were quite soft-edged lines, while the fuselage patterns seem to have been much more random and almost unique to each aircraft.

The top view is a Me109G-2 trop of LG2 serving in Sicily in 1943, topside Sandgelb 79 with fuselage mottled in Olivgrün 80, underside in Himmelblau 78, bottom cowl painted Gelb 04 and white theatre markings on the underside of the wing tips.

The second view shows a Me109 G-6 of J952 in Russia during 1943 with the top in soft-wedged camouflage in two shades of Graü 74 and 75 with a dappling of 74 and RLM02 down the fuselage sides theatre markings in yellow.

The third view shows a G70 of JG300 defending Germany in 1945 in a soft-edged camouflage in Olivgrün 80 and Braunviolett 81 and an underside in Weissblau 76.

The final view shows the k variant of JG77 in a similar scheme to that applied in view three.

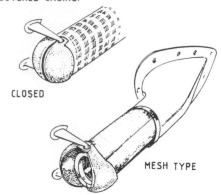

LOUVERED CASING.

CLOSED

MESH TYPE

TROPICAL OR SAND FILTER.

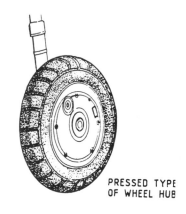

OIL PUMP COVER ON G5 & G14 MODELS ONLY.

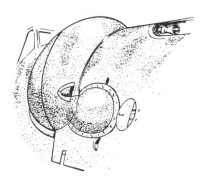

PRESSED TYPE OF WHEEL HUB

AERIAL ATTACHMENT TO FIN G2 MODEL.

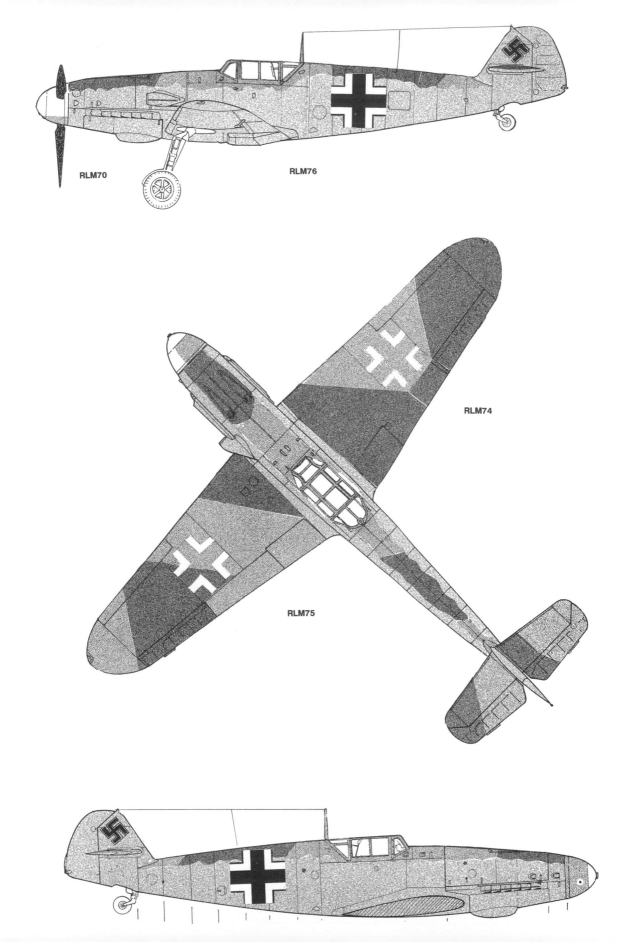

RLM70   RLM76

RLM74

RLM75

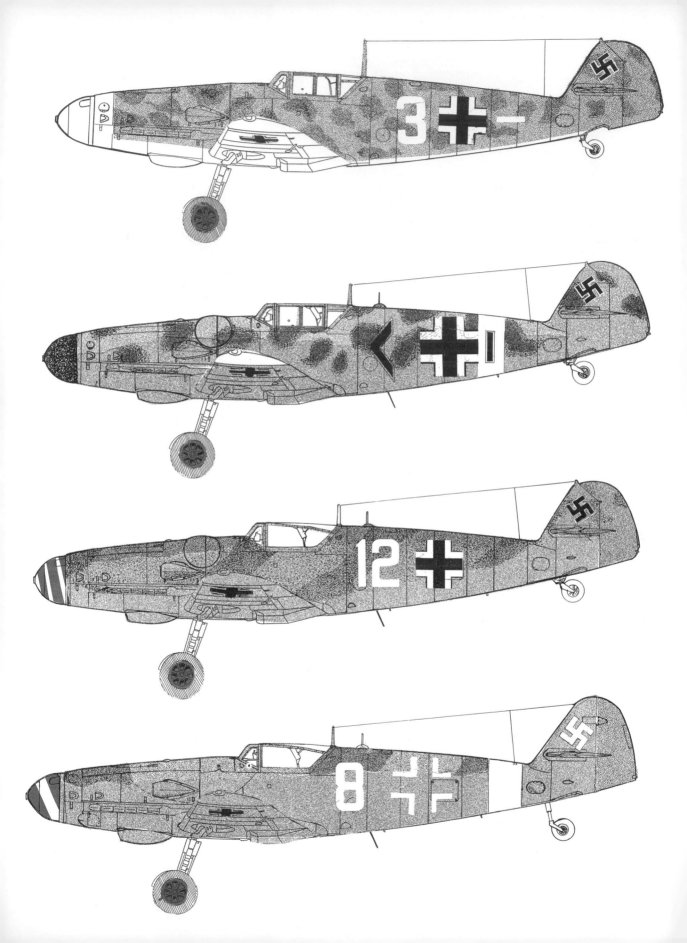

Messerschmitt Me210 and 410

Intended as a replacement for the Me110 which was increasingly proving its inadequacy as a long range escort machine, the Me210 proved one of Germany's greatest failures. It had poor longitudinal stability, readily dropping into an unwanted spin. Despite many substantial modifications, including increasing the length by some 3½ft, the improvement in performance was limited and the aircraft still incurred a high rate of loss through accidents. Although it was introduced in limited numbers on both the Eastern and Western Fronts, it never enjoyed any success often being replaced, gratefully, by its predecessor.

The lack of success and rapid withdrawal of the 210 type left a sizeable hole in the Luftwaffe armament inventory and, with so much effort put into setting up and producing the 210, one solution was to turn to the intended high altitude variant, the Me410, and develop this as the 110 replacement. The type was certainly an improvement on its sad predecessor but, by the time the 410 was introduced into service, the air war had changed into a daylight defence against the mass formations of US heavy bombers, escorted by ever increasing numbers of long range and manoeuvrable single engine escorts which the 410 could not match. It suffered accordingly with few notable successes such as the destruction of 34 four-engine US types which were downed without loss. The machine's lack of success as a heavy fighter led to a substantial number being deployed in the long range reconnaissance role operating from France and Norway.

Delivered in a 70/71/74 finish early in its career, the 210/410 followed the trends of other heavy fighter units. The three-view drawing shows such a scheme with heavy dapple on the fuselage top. The top side view shows the 210 in its limited service in August 1942. A similar scheme applied to the 410 variant is shown in side view two, but with the underside Grey carried much further up the fuselage sides.

The third view shows a reconnaissance machine operating over Italy in Light Grey 76 finish dappled with 75 overall on top and sides.

The final side view shows an aircraft serving in the defence of Germany in late 1944 and wearing a defined splinter finish in 74/75/76. Although the earlier bomber colours of Dark Green/Black Green with Blue undersides have been quoted, at this late stage of the War this now appears unlikely.

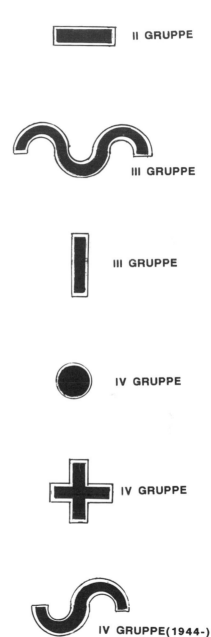

I GRUPPE

II GRUPPE

III GRUPPE

III GRUPPE

IV GRUPPE

IV GRUPPE

IV GRUPPE(1944-)

**GRUPPE IDENTIFICATION MARKINGS
CARRIED AFT OF NATIONAL MARKINGS**

31

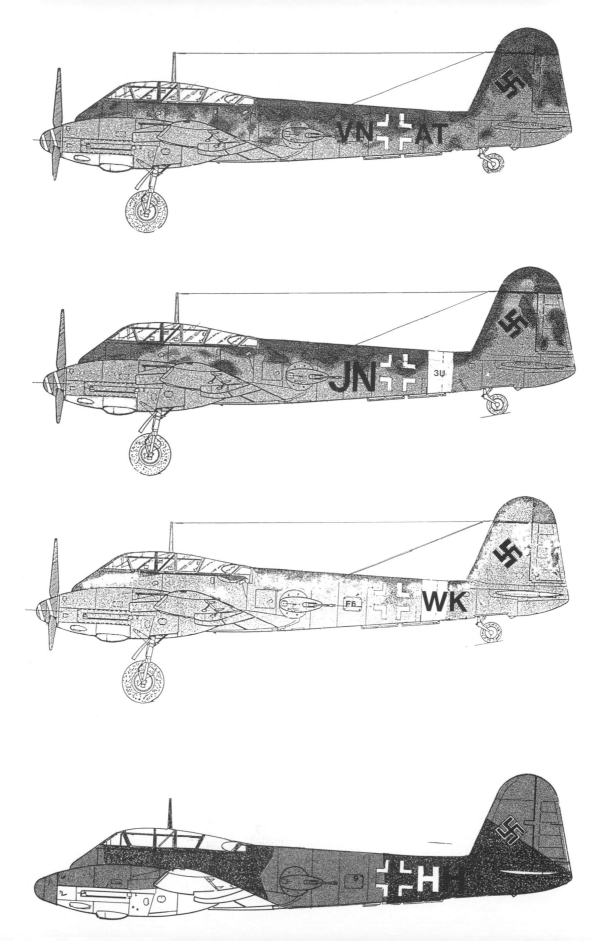

Heinkel He 219 UHU

Obviously, Ernst Heinkel did not share the German High Command's optimism for an early end to the War as, in 1940, he embarked part of his design team on producing an initial design as a replacement for Me110, Ju87, and Do17, using a single basic design to cover a number of roles. However, the submitted results met with no enthusiasm from the German Ministry of Aircraft Production and the idea was shelved. In 1941 Heinkel once again submitted his proposal, but it wasn't until the end of the year that a limited go-ahead for the night fighter version was given.

To make up for lost time, Heinkel manufactured the prototype in parallel with the detailed design, and pre-production machines were passed directly to a special front line unit for evaluation. Thus, on the night of June 11/12 1940, Major Strieb destroyed five Lancasters in his first sortie, while the rest of his squadron claimed to have shot down a total of twenty aircraft, including six Mosquitos.

The aircraft was received with great enthusiasm, but still an order requesting a production of 12 machines a month was all that was forthcoming, while General Milch, Head of Luftwaffe Procurement, was all in favour of cancelling the project in favour of well-tried, existing types, although these were blatantly inferior!

Once again, production was cancelled but, such was the demand from the front line units, Heinkel ignored the order but could only continue on a small scale so that, by the end of the War, a total of only 294 machines, which included six made up from spares, had been completed!

It can be seen that the UHU wasn't employed for long enough or in sufficiently large numbers for any great variation or development of paint schemes to take place. The majority of early machines appear to be finished in the overall pale Grey RLM 76, although some were initially in overall Black.

When introduced into service the basic scheme was, as shown in the three views, overall Grey 76 dappled with the darker Grey 74. Some evidence exists that on some aircraft RLM 76 replaced 74. This basic pattern could be applied to the top surfaces only as shown in the top side view of an aircraft G9 + FB of NJG 1. The mottling could only extend half-way down as shown in the second side view of an aircraft from the same unit, this time with Black sides and lower surface. The third unit shows an unusual colour scheme of a base Grey, probably 74, with a heavy scribble of RLM 76 over upper surfaces whilst sides and undersurfaces are again in Black. Our final view shows the basic overall mottle camouflage on an aircraft of 1/NJ3, but with a much finer dapple of the engine nacelles.

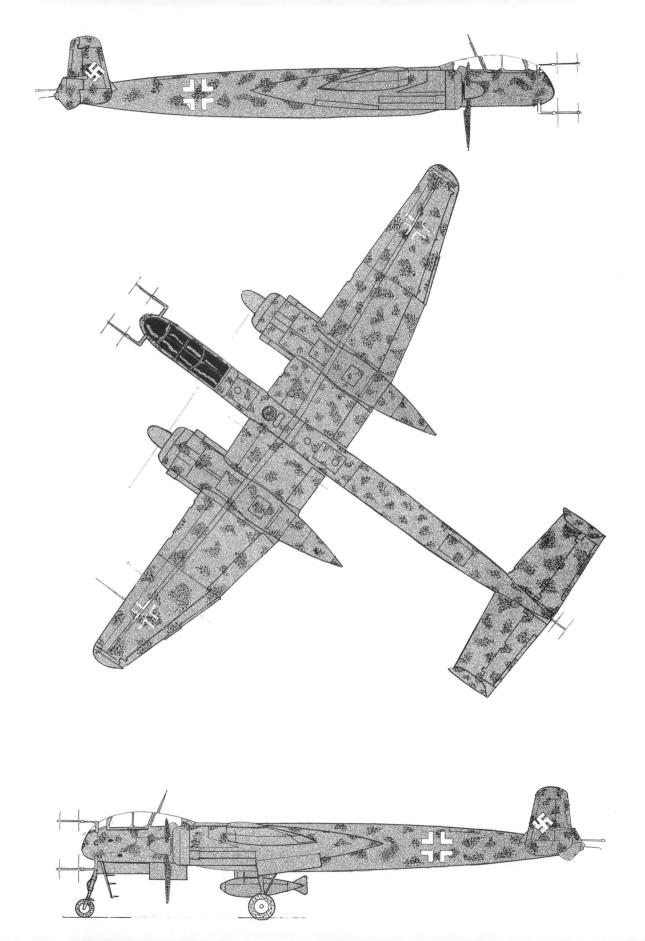

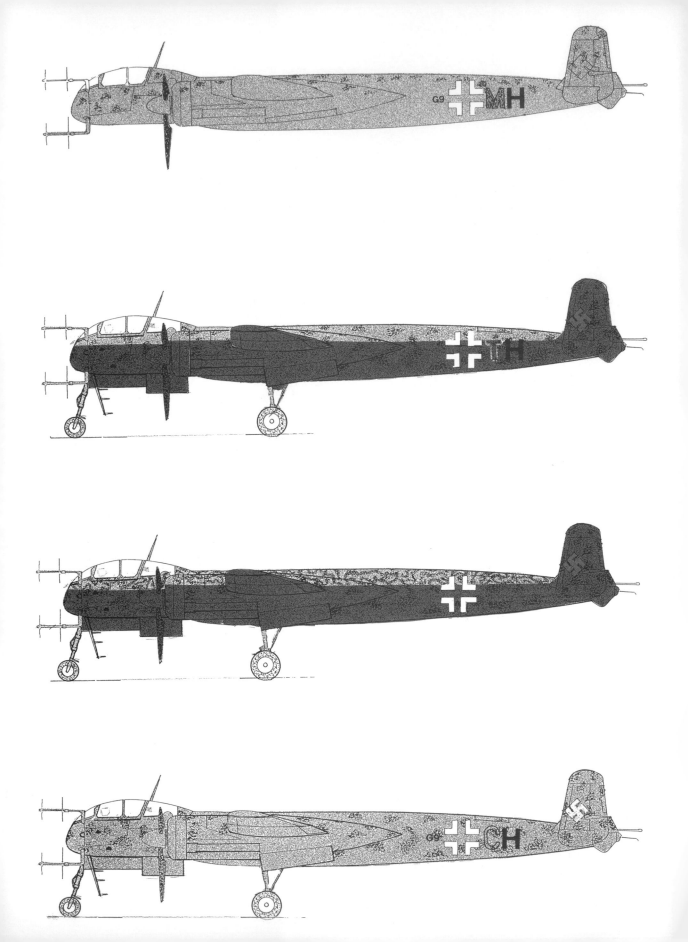

Focke Wulf FW 190D & TA152

Successful as it was, the basic FW190 was the subject of a programme to improve its qualities purely as a fighter, as against schemes to adapt the aircraft for other roles. When the Junkers Jumo 213 twelve-cylinder engine was considered as a replacement for the BMW motors, the resultant D variant became the most radical development, giving rise to a whole new type of 'long nose' aircraft.

So outstanding was the change, both visually and with regard to performance and potential, that the aircraft was redesignated in the autumn of 1943 as the TA152 series in honour of its designer Kurt Tank, although only subsequent types took this designation.

The introduction of the new engine not only gave a marked increase in performance, but also offered the possibility of producing a high-altitude interceptor variant, capable of tackling the latest pressurised bomber and reconnaissance Mosquitos and Spitfires, which up to then had intruded with virtual impunity. The resultant aircraft, with an even longer nose and high aspect ratio wings of some 48 ½ft, was not without snags, and not until the much-modified C version attained production did the type enter service at the end of 1944. Only one squadron, JG301, was fully equipped with this excellent machine by the end of the War, and teething troubles, supply problems and lack of fuel curtailed even this unit's activities.

As with the airframe of the FW190D which was a logical development of the earlier short nose variants, the colours applied to the long nose variant were in the standard 81/82/83 Greens of the 1944 period and painted in at least two distinctive patterns as shown in the small drawing. Further pattern developments were applied to accommodate the greater span of the TA152 as shown in the three-view diagram.

The top view depicts an aircraft prior to delivery with temporary manufacturer's four letter code on both the fuselage side and repeated beneath the wings.

The second side view shows an aircraft of JG54 which crash-landed at Wemmel in Jan 1945 while participating in the ill-fated last fling of the Luftwaffe's coded operation 'Bodenplatte' when the Germans made mass attacks on Allied airfields in the Low Countries. Surprisingly, it bears a Yellow rudder and lower engine cowl reminiscent of earlier Eastern Front theatre markings.

The third view shows an aircraft in unusually sharp-edged camouflaged and bearing Black and White Defence of the Reich bands around the rear fuselage.

The fourth side view depicts the final operational variant of the line, the TA152, which only saw operation with JG301 and bears that unit's red/yellow/red Defence of the Reich markings While the national markings are applied in dark Grey, an increasingly common practice during the closing months of the War. Dark Green was also used on some rare occasions, so careful research is needed for accurate reproduction of any particular machine.

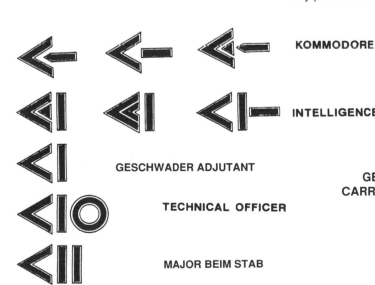

KOMMODORE

INTELLIGENCE OFFICER

GESCHWADER ADJUTANT

TECHNICAL OFFICER

MAJOR BEIM STAB

**GESCHWADER PILOT RANK MARKINGS
CARRIED FORWARD OF NATIONAL MARKINGS**

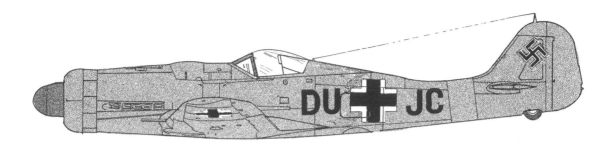

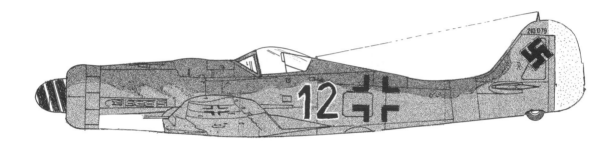

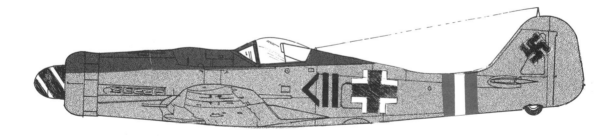

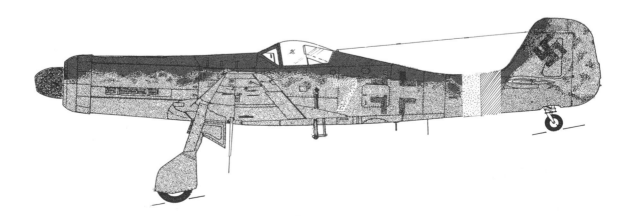

The Messerschmitt Me 262 'Schwalb'

In many ways, it is a great pity that the narrow outlook of the German Ministry of Aircraft Production, and political interference, blunted so much of Germany's inspired aeronautic design and production. These forces delayed and changed the introduction of the world's first operational jet fighter, which could have seen combat some twelve months before it actually did and in its intended role of fighter, not as a fairly ineffectual reprisal bomber.

When it did finally emerge in its intended role against the Allied day air offensive, it proved outstanding and only production problems with the quality of engines blighted its short career.

The advancing Allied armies meant that the airfields from which the 262 operated were now constantly under threat from shorter-range, low-altitude attacks.

Development of the aircraft proceeded apace with the introduction of R4M rockets, which were applied with devastating effect from outside the range of the US bombers' defensive fire.

Out of a production of 1,433 aircraft, only just over 100 actually saw active service.

The three-view drawing shows one of several apparently 'standard' schemes all generally in 81/82 or 83 top with Hellgrau 76 undersides, although some aircraft have been recorded with natural metal undersurfaces, no doubt due to lack of materials at this late period.

The top view shows an aircraft from the Industrie Shuts Schwarm I which was absorbed into Jv44 during the last weeks of the War.

The second side view is of an aircraft flown by Major Rudolf Sinner of the staff or 11/Jg7 with its blue/red Defence of the Reich tailband and soft edge 81/82 pattern camouflage mottled on and below the fin, and with a small Röt 4 with White outline below the unit badge on the nose.

The third side view is of the aircraft flown by the ace Heinz Bar while serving with III EJG2 and has a fuselage with the rear end mottled with 81 over the base of 83.

The fourth view shows a reconnaissance machine with the bulged fairings over the nose cameras and no guns. The fuselage has a black-edged white band around the nose and a heavy 81 mottle over a base of 83.

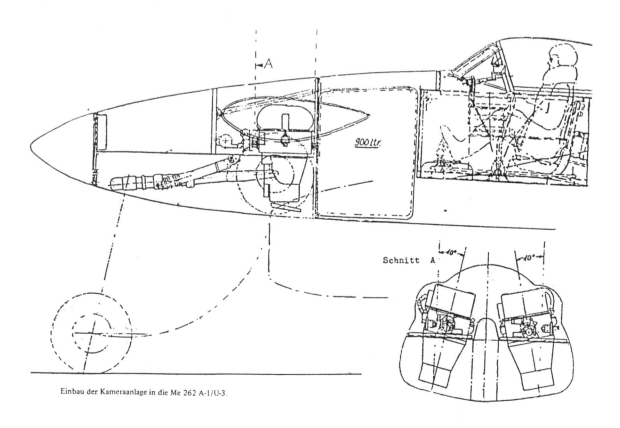

Einbau der Kameraanlage in die Me 262 A-1/U-3.

Schnitt A

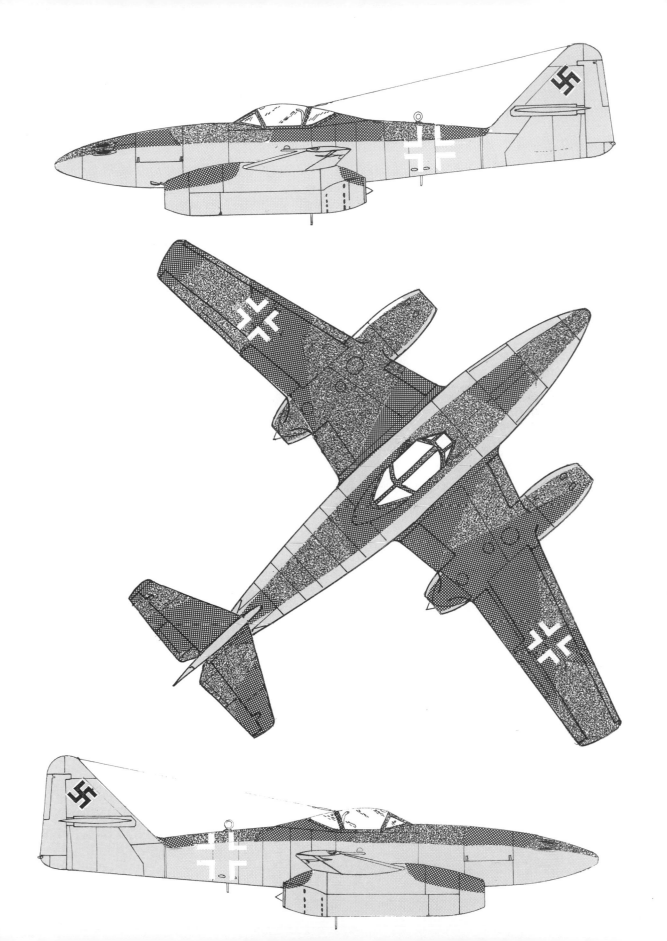

The Arado Ar234 'Blitz'

Although the 234 has the distinction of being the world's first jet bomber, it was only available in small quantities and its contribution made little impression on the Allied effort. Had the type been taken up, like many of the late German products, or indeed not been hindered at an earlier date, the Allies would have found their efforts much more costly.

As it was, the performance proved as embarrassing for the Allies as the introduction of the Mosquito had earlier been for the Germans. For the new jet bomber was able to operate with near impunity over Allied airspace, and even over the Eastern coast and harbours of England. Even with an external bomb load, the aircraft could fly either higher or faster than any of the defending fighters and, because of this, it was also used in the unarmed photo reconnaissance role during the autumn of 1944 and spring of 1945.

The Arado 234C series was basically similar to the B, but had four BMW 0034-1 turbojets, in place of the original pair of Junkers Jumo 004B motors. However, only nineteen of these production aircraft were in service before the end of hostilities, and none saw active service. Once again, it was a case of 'too little too late' for a very promising aircraft.

In 1944, RLM issued new instructions regarding colours for new aircraft types introducing the two greens 80/81 for top colours, with either blue green 83 on the underside of fighters or the blue grey shade 76 previously used on fighter undersides for bomber types.

As the Arado Jet Bomber was the only entirely new bomber type to be introduced during the closing stages of the War, this new scheme applied, and is depicted in the three-view drawing, although the actual splinter pattern was very similar to that introduced for bomber types at the outbreak of the War some five years earlier. The top side view takes this basic pattern and adds the operational unit markings of 8/Kg 76 - the only fully operational unit equipped with the bomber type. As the aircraft had no propeller spinners, the jet engine intake lips were often painted in the Stab colour, in this case Red. The aircraft was shot down while trying to destroy the Remagen Bridge.

The second side view shows the reconnaissance variant serving the Kommando Sperling and carrying two 300 Lt drop tanks, one under each engine cowling, but still wearing the original style and colour camouflage. Possibly due to the high level visibility of the standard colours at operational altitudes, or to lower the contrast between these colours and the wintery surfaces

of 44/45, several aircraft were crudely daubed in broad stripes of pale colour as seen on the third aircraft captured by the British in the closing weeks of the War.

Because of its outstanding performance, it was a logical step to convert the aircraft to a night fighter and a few machines saw limited operational evaluation sorties mounted with cannon packs under the aircraft belly. A move of a similar desperate solution was undertaken by the British with the Blenheim in 1940! With a more fighter style mottle finish over the fuselage, this aircraft which served with NJ1 is shown in our final side view.

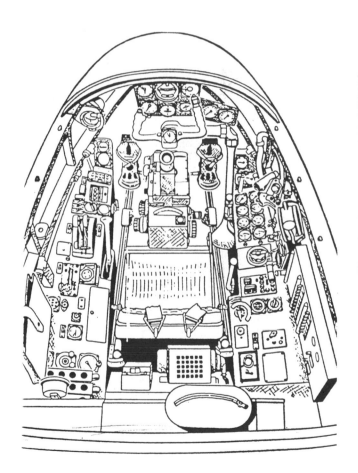

RLM65

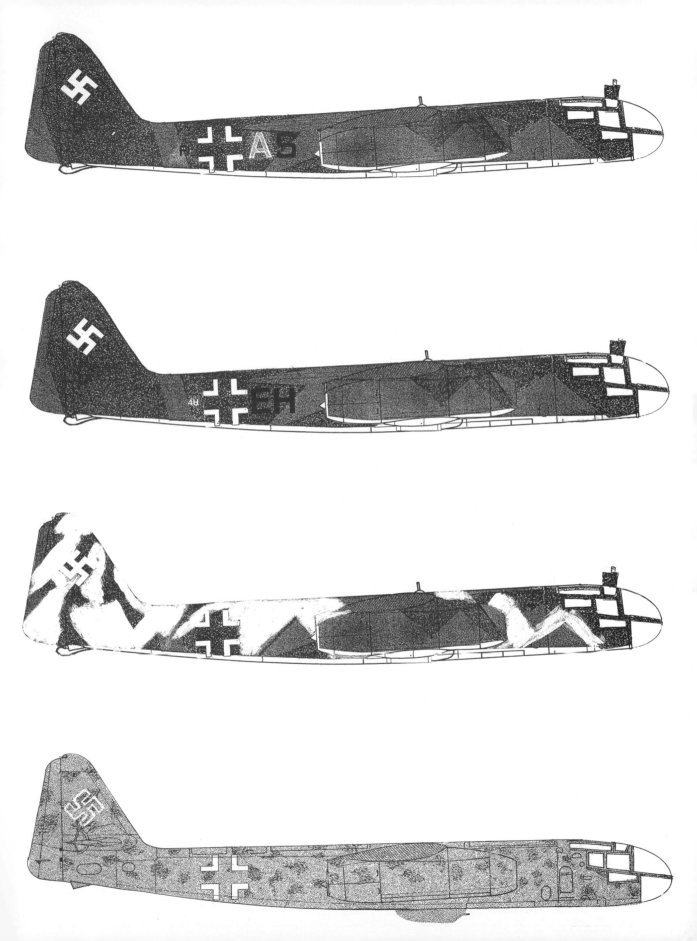

The Messerschmitt Me163 'Komet'

This remarkable little plane was an inspired answer to the problem of providing a point defence fighter to combat the American bomber formations then intruding, with ever greater impunity, over German targets. The problem was not only to penetrate the defensive fire of the masses of 50in machine guns able to concentrate on any area of the surrounding sky, but also to get through the American fighter escorts which were appearing in greater numbers and deeper into occupied air space, and now accompanying the bombers all the way to the target.

The 'Komet's' answer to both problems was to provide a small frontal area for the defensive gunners to shoot at, and a high speed capability to evade the American fighters. The aircraft was not without its drawbacks, however, and the instability, combined with the toxic and corrosive qualities of the liquid fuel used in the Walther rocket motor, caused more losses than enemy action, especially as there was a distinct tendency for any amount left over at the end of the motor burn to explode when landing on the aircraft skid. Such problems delayed the introduction of the aircraft into combat until late

1944 and, fortunately for the bombers of the US 8th Air Force, it did not see extensive service, while rapidly dwindling facilities and resources kept the larger 'C' development, with a more powerful rocket motor, out of production until too late to see any service.

Like so many revolutionary German types, one wonders what the outcome would have been had not apathy and interference stopped their earlier commitment to the conflict.

The top view shows the prototype in its distinctive overall red finish, while the three-view drawing shows one of two definitive camouflage patterns, recorded both in soft-edged 81/82 but with undersides in 83.

This is reflected in the second of our side view drawings which depicts a machine of KG400 the main user of the type.

The third view shows a more subtle finish applied to many aircraft with soft mottle finish in several greens, some now standard, over the entire fuselage and fin. A number of aircraft have been recorded being finished in the older two Grey top and pale grey undersides as depicted in the fourth illustration.

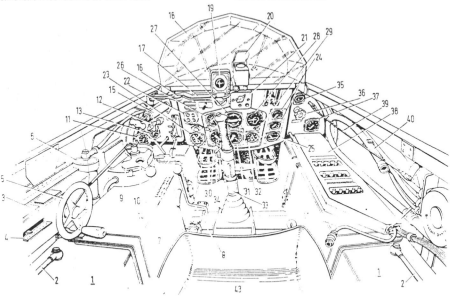

1. 'T-STOFF' TANK EACH SIDE OF COCKPIT.	12. U/C SELECTOR VALVE.	22. U/C POSITION INDICATOR.	33. CONTROL COLUMN.
2. FUEL FEED PIPES.	13. COMPRESSED AIR GAUGE.	23. CLOCK.	34. MK 108 CHARGING KNOB.
3. TRIM CONTROL BOX.	14. SKID POSITION SELECTOR.	24. THRUST INDICATORS.	35. OXYGEN INDICATOR.
4. TRIM ADJUSTMENT INDICATOR.	15. QUICK DUMP FOR FUEL.	25. TEMPERATURE GAUGE.	36. OXYGEN REGULATOR.
5. TRIMMER HANDWHEEL.	16. CANOPY LATCH.	26. AIRSPEED INDICATOR.	37. OXYGEN PRESSURE GAUGE.
6. OIL PRESSURE RESERVOIR.	17. CANOPY RELEASE.	27. ARTIFICIAL HORIZON	38. RADIO PANEL.
7. FLAP SELECTOR LEVER.	18. 90mm ARMOUR GLASS.	28. VARIOMETER.	39. EMERGENCY CANOPY RELEASE.
8. FLAP HAND PUMP.	19. COMPASS.	29. FUEL CONTENTS 'TELL-TALE'	40. PILOT'S OXYGEN PIPE.
9. THROTTLE QUADRANT.	20. REVI 16 REFLECTOR	30. ALTIMETER.	41. HELMET/RADIO LEAD.
10. STARTER SWITCH	GUNSIGHT.	31. R.P.M. COUNTER.	42. OXYGEN SUPPLY OUTLET.
11. U/C SYSTEM PRESSURE GAUGE.	21. FuG 25a CONTROL BOX.	32. CONSUMPTION INDICATOR.	43. SEAT, (ADJUSTABLE).

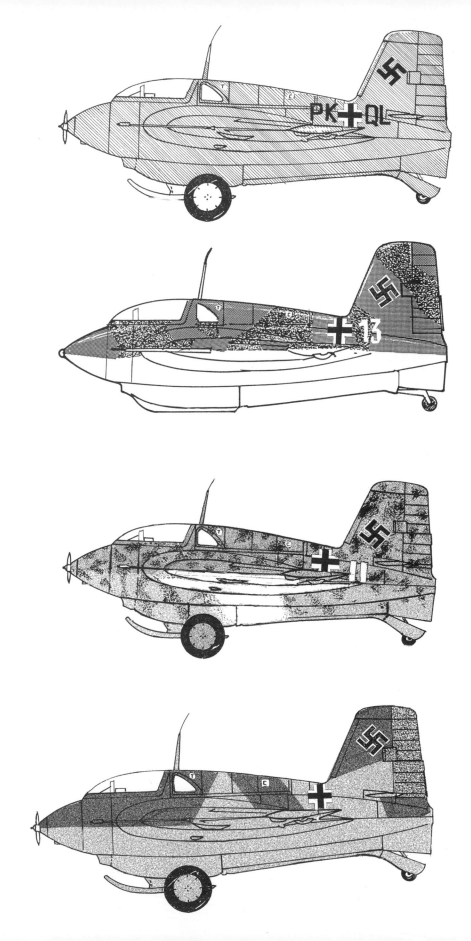

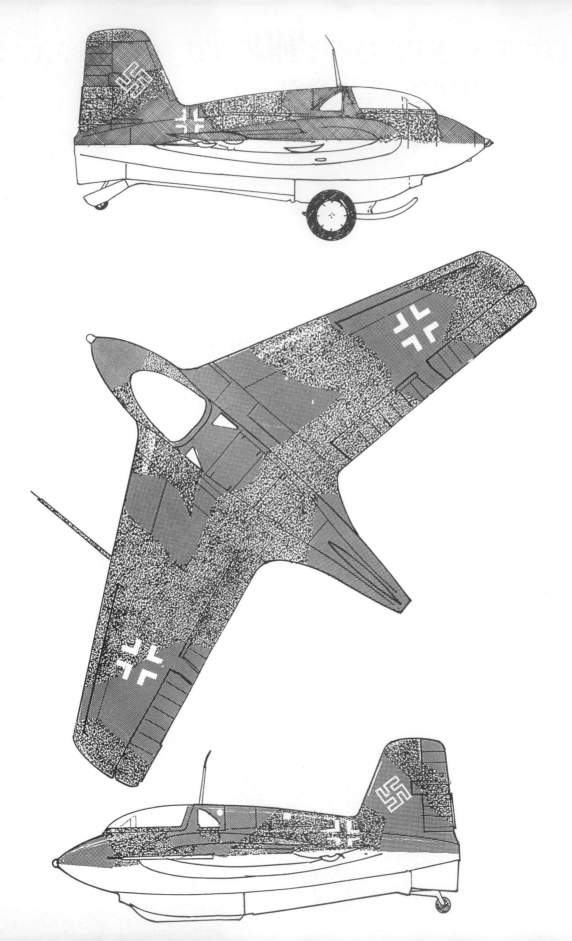